The Care and Feeding of DiNoSAURS

TIMOTHY J. BRADLEY

THE MILLBROOK PRESS
BROOKFIELD, CONNECTICUT

For Kayellen and Ryan

Published by The Millbrook Press, Inc.
2 Old New Milford Road
Brookfield, CT 06804
www.millbrookpress.com

Text and illustrations copyright © 2000 by Timothy J. Bradley
Printed in Hong Kong

The author takes full responsibility for the accuracy of the text, and gratefully acknowledges Clint McKnight of the Dinosaur Nature Association in Utah for his review of the manuscript.
E-mail the author at Raptoryx13@aol.com

Library of Congress Cataloging-in-Publication Data
Bradley, Timothy J.
The care and feeding of dinosaurs / Timothy J. Bradley.—
A Millbrook Press Library ed.
p. cm.
Includes bibliographical references (p.).
Summary: Speculates about what it would be like to have a dinosaur as a pet and provides information about specific species and the time periods in which they lived.
ISBN 0-7613-1305-2 (lib. bdg.)
1. Dinosaurs—Juvenile literature.
[1. Dinosaurs.]
I. Title.
QE862.D5 B63 2000
567.9—dc21
99-087564   CIP   AC

ABOUT THE ART

The dinosaurs in this book have been depicted with bright colors and bold patterns on their skins. Since color is something that doesn't fossilize like bones, no one is certain what colors dinosaurs were. But their modern-day ancestors —reptiles and birds—come in an amazing array of colors and patterns. Color can help with camouflage, mating displays, and expressing emotions like anger or fear.

It makes sense to think that color may have played an important part in a dinosaur's life, as well. Since dinosaurs are considered to have been active, agile animals, I feel that their colors and patterns might have been as interesting as the animals themselves were.

What would it be like to have a DINOSAUR for a PET?

DIPLODOCUS

Wait a minute! Everyone knows that dinosaurs don't exist anymore. They disappeared millions and millions and millions of years ago! The last dinosaurs died a long time before humans ever lived on Earth. No one has ever seen a live dinosaur. In fact, the only way that we even know that dinosaurs existed is because people have found traces of them in the ground—their bones, teeth, footprints, and even their poop. These traces of dinosaurs were buried so long they became fossilized, which made them become as hard as stone.

To picture what dinosaurs were like when they lived, paleontologists (people who study dinosaurs and other prehistoric life forms) use their imaginations to make sense of all the fossil traces left behind. They can figure out how big some dinosaurs were, what some of them liked to eat, and how fast others could run. To picture what it would be like to have a dinosaur for a pet, you'll need to use *your* imagination!

3

Where do BABY DINOSAURS come from?

TITANOSAURUS

The same as today's birds and reptiles, most baby dinosaurs hatched from eggs. Preserved dinosaur nests with eggs and eggshells have been found in many parts of the world. Some of those eggs contain fossilized baby dinosaurs.

Eggs protect the baby inside and also contain enough food for the baby to grow. The eggshell also lets air in, so the baby can get oxygen. But, even though eggs are good protection, they still can use some looking after. They need to be kept warm, but not too warm, and they need shelter from things like bad weather and animals that might like to eat them. A dry, sandy nest with a layer of leaves and twigs over the eggs might have done nicely—the sand would hold the sun's heat, and as the top layer of leaves rotted, it would produce heat, as well as provide shade. Small dinosaur moms might have sat right on top of their eggs, like chickens do today.

How long will my DINOSAUR need to stay in a NEST?

Some baby dinosaurs, like these *Hypacrosaurus* (hy-PAK-ro-SAWR-us) hatchlings, might need lots of care and attention. How can we know that? Fossilized nests of these dinosaurs contain eggshells that were crushed into tiny pieces. Scientists think this means that the hatchlings stayed in the nest for a long time, crushing their eggshells underfoot as they scrambled for food or nestled close for nap time.

Orodromeus (or-oh-DRO-me-us) babies were probably ready to leave their nest before *Hypacrosaurus* babies. Eggshells found in *Orodromeus* nests were in larger pieces. That could be because they left the nest soon after hatching, and didn't spend as much time toddling around their nest.

Your dinosaur will spend some time in the nest eating, sleeping, and growing. It could be for as little as a week or as long as several months. It might be a good idea to find a dependable dinosaur-sitter so you don't become nest bound. When your dinosaur is ready it will leave the nest for good and begin to explore the world around it.

HYPACROSAURUS

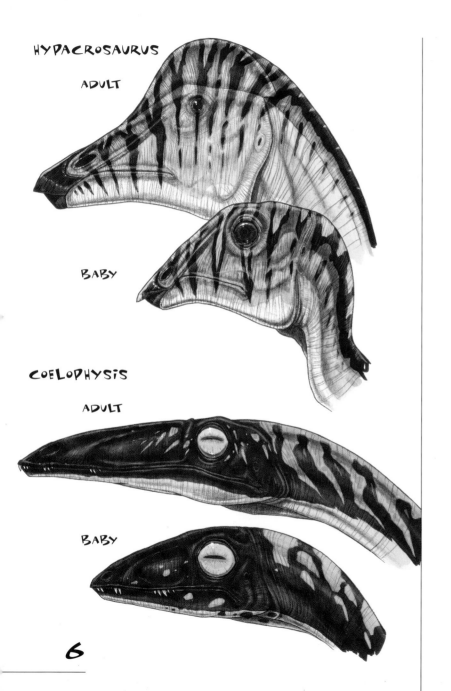

HYPACROSAURUS

ADULT

BABY

COELOPHYSIS

ADULT

BABY

What would a BABY DINOSAUR LOOK like?

Baby dinosaurs are cute, aren't they? Their heads and eyes are bigger and rounder than their parents' are. Puppies and kittens and human babies have facial features like that too. The special way babies look makes you want to cuddle and protect them. Some scientists think that animal parents (this includes humans!) have brains that are made to love and take care of their babies. That way, the adults will protect the babies, and give them a better chance to have babies of their own. Being a good parent to your babies makes sense for every animal.

Another way baby dinosaurs might have grabbed some attention is with sounds—anyone with a younger sister or brother will understand that. Baby birds will sit in the nest with their mouths wide open and chirp until they get a nice juicy worm. Baby dinosaurs may have had special cries or honks that were so noisy the parents would have to give them something to eat.

What would be *GOOD* to *FEED* my *BABY DINOSAUR?*

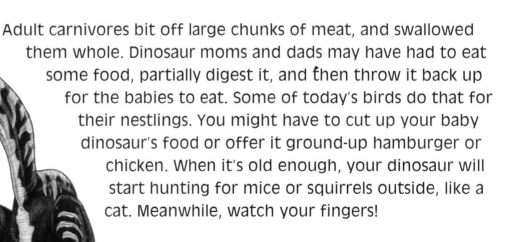

MAIASAURA

That all depends on what kind of dinosaur you have chosen as a pet. The *Maiasaura* (MY-ah-SAWR-ah) is an herbivore. She eats only plants. Her parents may have fed her partially digested plants, so you might put some leaves and berries into a blender to make them easier for the baby to eat.

Some dinosaurs, like the *Coelophysis* (seel-oh-FY-sis) baby, are carnivores, or meat-eaters. When it is still little, it may not be able to eat the same way that the adult dinosaurs eat, thankfully. Dinosaur teeth were not made for chewing, like ours are.

Adult carnivores bit off large chunks of meat, and swallowed them whole. Dinosaur moms and dads may have had to eat some food, partially digest it, and then throw it back up for the babies to eat. Some of today's birds do that for their nestlings. You might have to cut up your baby dinosaur's food or offer it ground-up hamburger or chicken. When it's old enough, your dinosaur will start hunting for mice or squirrels outside, like a cat. Meanwhile, watch your fingers!

COELOPHYSIS

How much PROTECTION would a BABY DINOSAUR need?

Since this baby *Hypacrosaurus* wouldn't leave the nest for some time, it may have had a covering of hair or feathers to protect it from the sun and the rain. After it has hatched, keep it in a sturdy box with a blanket, shredded newspaper, or even leaves and twigs until the baby gets old enough to walk around on its own.

Since paleontologists think *Orodromeus* babies could leave their nests soon after hatching, they wouldn't need to be born with insulation—they could explore to find protection from the weather. If you want a more independent dinosaur, which will be ready to play soon after hatching, *Orodromeus* may be a good choice for you.

ORODROMEUS

HYPACROSAURUS

8

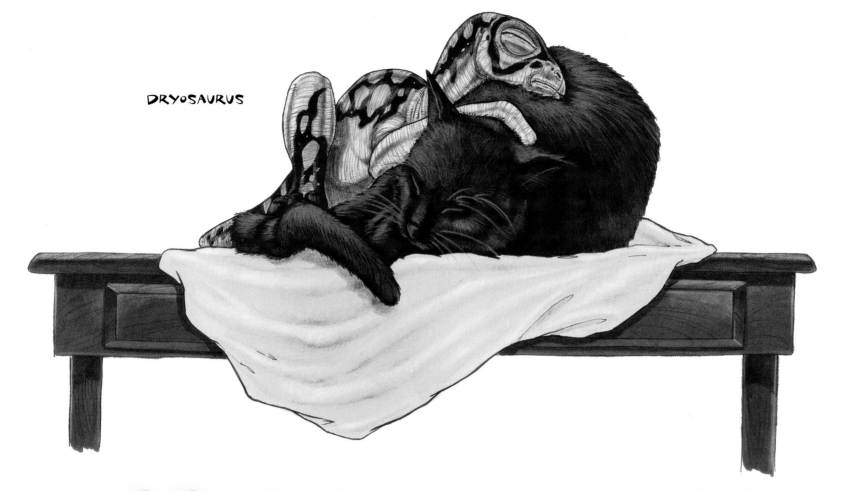

DRYOSAURUS

Would a BABY DINOSAUR get along with my OTHER PETS?

Possibly, if they were raised together, like this kitten and *Dryosaurus* (DRY-oh-SAWR-us) baby. That way, as your pets grow up together, they will be used to being around each other. Some dinosaurs might get lonely after being separated from their brothers and sisters, so they might enjoy the warmth and companionship that a kitten or puppy would provide. However, some baby dinosaurs that are more independent right from birth might see a puppy or kitten as a threat.

How FAST do DINOSAURS grow?

Some dinosaurs grew very quickly compared to modern-day animals. Even the biggest dinosaurs, the largest animals ever to live on Earth, may have become fully grown in fifteen or twenty years. How do paleontologists know that? They can estimate by counting "growth rings" in the fossilized bones, in the same way the growth rings in a tree stump can be counted to know how old it was.

TYRANNOSAURUS

MAIASAURA

ADULT   BABY   JUVENILE

Did DINOSAURS like the WATER?

Scientists used to think that sauropod (SAWR-o-pod) dinosaurs (a type that walked on all four legs, had small heads at the end of really long necks, and long tails), like this young *Brachiosaurus* (brak-ee-oh-SAWR-us), spent all their time in swamps because they were so heavy. Scientists thought these huge creatures could not support their own weight on land, and needed to float in the water to keep their bones from breaking. Also, their teeth seemed too fragile to eat anything tougher than mushy water plants. Now pale-ontologists think that sauropods spent most of their time on dry land, only going into the water to cool off, like elephants do today. Fossils of these dinosaurs

BRACHiOSAURUS

have been found in areas where there was not a lot of water during the time they lived. So if you choose a sauropod for a pet, get a pool and be prepared to share it.

13

COMPSOGNATHUS

Should I give my DINOSAUR A BATH?

Trying to get your dinosaur to take a bath in the tub would be pretty tricky if it didn't want to. It might be a better idea to have a birdbath out in your yard to help your dinosaur keep cool and clean. A dinosaur like little *Compsognathus* (comp-so-NAY-thus) might like to splash around a bit.

Other dinosaurs might like to take a dust bath. Lots of modern-day animals do that too. A good roll in the dirt would help protect your dinosaur's skin from the hot sun and bugs, and scratch those hard-to-reach itches. Dinosaurs that lived in hot, dry areas, like *Velociraptor* (ve-LOSS-ih-RAP-ter) might enjoy that.

Did DINOSAURS take NAPS?

Carnivorous dinosaurs like *Coelophysis* hunted their own food, and that burns up a lot of energy. In order to save that energy for catching dinner, meat-eaters probably spent most of the time napping in the sun until the time was right to start looking for a bite to eat. Modern-day lions spend almost all day sleeping or resting, and only use a couple of hours actually chasing down prey.

If you've chosen a carnivorous dinosaur as your pet, expect it to spend much of the day in a nice, comfortable resting spot.

COELOPHYSIS

TROODON

How WELL could DiNOSAURS SEE?

Good eyesight was important for helping the dinosaurs find food. Dinosaur eyes were positioned in different ways, depending on whether they were carnivores or herbivores. Meat-eaters needed keen vision to hunt their prey. Their eyes pointed forward, so they could judge distances better.

Plant-eaters had eyes on the sides of their heads, so they could see potential danger more easily, not to mention new food sources.

TiTANOSAURUS

Could DINOSAURS SEE in COLOR?

This young *Lambeosaurus* (lam-bee-o-SAWR-us) has found a nice snack—a flowerpot full of bright, colorful pansies. Paleontologists have found fossilized molds of the brains of some dinosaurs. The size and structure of some dinosaur brains indicates that they had well-developed eyes, which were able to see colors.

What good is color vision? Some dinosaurs may have been brightly colored or had bold skin patterns, which could be used as signals to other dinosaurs—for communication among members of a herd, or as a warning to other kinds of dinosaurs to keep away. It is possible that some dinosaurs may have had the ability to change colors depending on their emotions the way that modern-day chameleons can.

Your dinosaur may react to color in an unpredictable way—it may take a while before you understand which colors cause a reaction. Meanwhile, don't be surprised if it gets mad at your pants.

LAMBEOSAURUS

17

PARASAUROLOPHUS

Would a DINOSAUR know how to GATHER iTS OWN FOOD once it leaves the nest?

It might be necessary to help your dinosaur learn a few tricks. Dinosaurs probably had lots of instinctual behaviors built into their brains, but like many young animals they needed their parents to show them the right way to do some things. Plant-eaters would need to learn where to get the best leaves, and meat-eaters would need some lessons on hunting skills. Many animals learn how to survive just by playing when they are young. They play-fight with their siblings and play at copying what their older brothers and sisters do.

Would DiNOSAURS have FUN playing WiTH TOYS?

Some scientists think that dinosaurs were lively, energetic animals. Playing with toys might provide stimulation for your pet's brain and exercise for its muscles. Plant-eaters would be curious about a brightly colored ball, and might enjoy rolling it around. However, don't expect them to get the hang of a game of "fetch." Most dinosaur brains were very small, and even the simple game of fetch would be too much for them to learn. Some of the meat-eating dinosaurs, like *Velociraptor*, spent lots

VELOCiRAPTOR

of time and energy hunting for food. They might like toys that they could chase. Running and pouncing skills need to be practiced for the time when your carnivorous dinosaur decides to start catching its own dinner.

19

Should my DINOSAUR be free to WANDER AROUND my neighborhood?

It would probably be a good idea to put a fence around your yard when your dinosaur is old enough to be out on its own. She will need some space to get exercise, and a fence will protect your dinosaur and your neighbors. Your mailman will be very grateful.

When they're old enough, small meat-eating dinosaurs like *Compsognathus* will enjoy running around outside to hunt for mice and squirrels. Bigger dinosaurs will be on the lookout for bigger morsels—make sure the neighborhood pets (and the neighbors!) are safe in their houses so they won't become a snack for a frisky *Tyrannosaurus* (ty-RAN-oh-SAWR-us).

VELOCIRAPTOR

Why do some DiNOSAURS have CLAWS?

To a predatory dinosaur like *Velociraptor*, claws are very important for catching prey. Other dinosaurs like the giant sauropods would have used their claws for defense against predators or for traction to help them walk in sand or mud. Your dinosaur might try to sharpen its claws on the furniture, like cats do. You may want to provide a scratching post.

VELOCIRAPTOR

What about when my DINOSAUR needs to GO TO THE BATHROOM?

Housebreaking your dinosaur will be a difficult thing to do. When dinosaurs lived they could poop anywhere they wanted and nobody had to clean up after them. The small dinosaur brain cannot understand why pooping on the living room rug is not okay (and with a big dinosaur like *Apatosaurus* (a-PAT-oh-sawr-us) we're talking about a lot of poop). You cannot expect any wild animal to understand the rules of your house. It has taken thousands of years to domesticate dogs and cats, and they still make mistakes.

APATOSAURUS

23

Some dinosaurs, both carnivorous and
herbivorous, appear to have lived in groups.
Scientists have found fossilized groups of
dinosaurs such as *Coelophysis* and *Centrosaurus*
(SEN-tro-SAWR-us) where it appeared
many individuals had gathered
together for some reason.
Also, trackways of fossilized
footprints made by many
different-sized sauropod
dinosaurs have been found,

CHASMOSAURUS

24

possibly indicating that they were traveling in a herd like elephants do today. A ceratopsian (ser-a-TOP-see-an: horned dinosaur) like *Chasmosaurus* (KAZ-mo-sawr-us) might feel comfortable grazing with a herd of cattle. For plant-eating dinosaurs, living in a herd would provide better protection for each of the individual animals. They could also defend the babies in the herd more effectively.

For meat-eaters, living as part of a pack, like wolves do, makes hunting easier. All the adults cooperate to hunt their prey and they all share it.

How much ROOM would a GROWN-UP DINOSAUR need?

A teenaged *Carnotaurus* (kar-no-TOR-us) is having fun chasing after some sheep she found in a nearby field. Even if you keep your big meat-eaters well fed, they will still try to hunt whenever they can. To keep them from munching on other people's animals, not to mention other people, you might want to buy someplace like a cattle ranch. There would be lots of room and lots to chase, and people will stay away from a field that has a large, hungry dinosaur roaming about.

If you decide on one of the duck-billed hadrosaurs (HAD-ro-sawrs) or a long-necked sauropod for your pet dinosaur, a few hundred acres of rain forest would be nice.

CARNOTAURUS

27

Would my DINOSAUR ever GET ANGRY?

Probably not the way people do, but it may have some built-in reactions. Territorialism (claiming an area as your own) may have been a trait of dinosaurs. Dinosaurs may have marked their territory with special scent glands, like many modern-day animals. This could be to protect a source of food or a nest. A fossilized *Protoceratops* (pro-toe-SER-a-tops) was found locked together with a *Velociraptor*. Scientists think that the *Protoceratops* may have been protecting its nest from the predator whose arm was caught in the *Protoceratops*'s mouth.

To keep other animals away, your dinosaur may try to look threatening by bobbing its head, or sound frightening by roaring. It may physically bump or attack a potential rival to drive it away or show who's boss.

Trying to figure out your dinosaur's mood will be difficult. Dinosaurs have fewer facial muscles than dogs or cats or people. Most of the muscles on the head of this *Allosaurus* (AL-oh-SAWR-us) are geared toward operating its jaws to give it a strong bite. It had lips that it could have pulled back to show its teeth, like a dog does to appear fierce. If your dinosaur looks at you like that, it might be a good idea to leave.

ALLOSAURUS

STEGOCERAS

29

What are those SPIKES on my DINOSAUR for?

Many dinosaurs had very strange body parts that scientists are still trying to understand. *Stegosaurus* (STEG-oh-SAWR-us) had big plates on its back. *Spinosaurus* (SPINE-oh-SAWR-us) had a huge sail growing on its back, and *Triceratops* (tri-SER-a-tops) had horns growing on its head. What good would those be? Scientists believe that sails or plates might have been useful for warming or cooling the dinosaur, and that horns were used for defense or attack. It is also possible that some features were used as a way to signal each other how they were feeling. Sails and plates could help a frightened dinosaur look bigger to an attacker. A modern-day frilled lizard uses its frill for the same purpose.

STEGOSAURUS

SPINOSAURUS

TRICERATOPS

31

BRACHIOSAURUS

How BiG will my DiNOSAUR be?

Dinosaurs come in an amazing range of sizes. A fully grown *Compsognathus* would be the size of a big chicken, small enough to hold in your lap (although it might not like that). An adult *Velociraptor* would be about the size of a wolf, and a grown-up *Brachiosaurus* would be big enough for you and all your friends to ride on. They had thirty-five-foot-long necks and weighed about fifty tons. They were huge. A *Tyrannosaurus* would be not only big but possibly very fast. They reached about forty feet long and weighed about five tons. Some paleontologists who have studied fossilized tyrannosaur leg bones think it may have been able to run as fast as a racehorse. Racing *Tyrannosaurs* would be fun and fast, but keep everyone out of the way, because once that five tons was moving, it would be hard to stop. Training them would be tough too, since you would always be in danger of being eaten while you were trying to break them in.

BRACHIOSAURUS

33

What kind of APPETITE will a GROWN-UP DINOSAUR have?

Sauropod dinosaurs, like this *Omeisaurus* (OH-mee-SAWR-us), have long necks and long balancing tails that allowed them to reach far for the best food. An adult sauropod will have to spend most of every day eating to produce enough energy for its huge body. This must have been difficult to do. Since the heads of sauropods were so small compared to the size of their bodies, they would only be able to eat a small mouthful of food with each bite, so lots of energy must have gone into taking lots of bites. Think about eating a big bowl of cereal with a baby spoon and you can see the problem.

OMEISAURUS

ALLOSAURUS

Paleontologists disagree about whether some dinosaur predators actively hunted for food or simply looked around for an already-dead animal to eat. It could be that they did a little of both. If you have a carnivore as your pet, you'll find out. The head of a meat-eater like *Allosaurus* is built to rip big chunks of meat from its prey and the swallow them without chewing. Carnivores did not have cheeks, which help hold food in your mouth while you are chewing it. All those big chunks would land in the dinosaur's stomach to be digested.

After a big meal a carnivorous dinosaur would probably look for a nice cozy spot to take a long nap. The hood of a car warmed by the afternoon sun might make the perfect place. Make sure you have plenty of food for yourself because a trip to the grocery store may have to wait for a few days.

What do dinosaurs DRINK?

Every living thing needs water. If you don't put out a bowl for your dinosaur, he'll find some on his own. And once your dinosaur gets thirsty, he won't be too picky where the water comes from.

COELOPHYSIS

Just how LONG will I HAVE my DINOSAUR?

It might be a good idea to keep a copy of this book to give to your grandchildren—you'll need help taking care of your dinosaur when you're ninety. Scientists don't know how long dinosaurs lived, but if we look at some animals around today we can see that some live as long as or longer than humans. Parrots can live for seventy years and some tortoises can live for over one hundred years! Since dinosaurs are related to both reptiles and birds, a long life span may be possible—in some cases 150 years or more. You will be able to grow old with your dinosaur and enjoy this amazing creature for a lifetime and more.

DICRAEOSAURUS

39

The word dinosaur comes from two Greek words—deinos, meaning "terrifying," and sauros, meaning "lizard." They probably would be terrifying live and up close, but they are not lizards. They are a special group of animals that are considered reptiles but also have some things in common with birds. They existed on Earth long ago during a time we call the Mesozoic (me-so-ZO-ic) Era. The Mesozoic Era is broken down into three parts: the Triassic (Try-AS-sic) Period, the Jurassic (Jur-AS-sic) Period, and the Cretaceous (cra-TAY-shus) Period. The last dinosaurs died out at the end of the Cretaceous Period, around 65 million years ago.

Throughout the Mesozoic Era, dinosaurs spread all over the world. It was much warmer than today, so even the polar regions supported dinosaurs.

TRIASSIC JURASS

Tyrannosaurus rex once lived in the United States of America. Its relative, *Albertosaurus*, has been uncovered in Canada, and another *T. rex* relation, *Tarbosaurus*, has been found in Mongolia. How did that happen? During the time of the dinosaurs, the major land masses were connected. As the continents slowly separated, the dinosaurs were not able to cross to another land mass, and over millions of years, evolved to fit their environments better. If you live in Colorado, and were able to go back to the Cretaceous era to visit, you might see *Triceratops* and *Tyrannosaurus* stalking around. In the Texas area during the Triassic era, you could see flocks of *Coelophysis*. Don't forget the sunscreen and a hat—it's going to be a hot, sunny day.

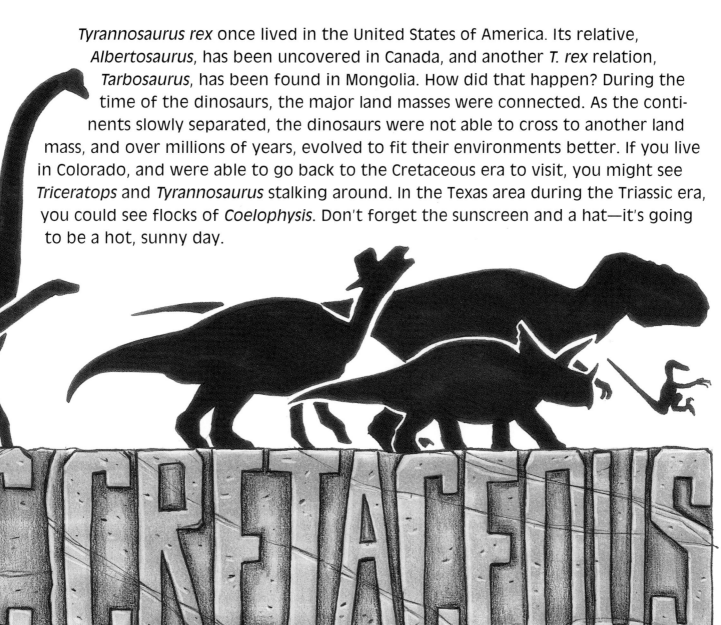

During the Triassic Period (about 245 to 208 million years ago), there were creatures like *Coelophysis*, *Plateosaurus* (PLATE-ee-oh-SAWR-us), and *Herrerasaurus* (ha-RARE-uh-SAWR-us).

COELOPHYSIS   PLATEOSAURUS   HERRERASAURUS

40-50 FEET

15 FEET

In the Jurassic Period (about 208 to 146 million years ago) new species of dinosaurs evolved, many growing to amazing size, like *Apatosaurus*, *Allosaurus*, *Brachiosaurus*, and *Stegosaurus*.

APATOSAURUS   ALLOSAURUS   BRACHIOSAURUS   STEGOSAURUS

ASSIC DINOSAURS

During the Cretaceous Period (about 146 to 65 million years ago), dinosaurs continued to thrive all over the world and there were many new species, like the fierce dinosaurs called *Velociraptors*, *Hypacrosaurus*, *Albertosaurus*, *Tyrannosaurus*, and *Lambeosaurus*.

20 FEET

3 FEET

VELOCIRAPTOR   HYPACROSAURUS   ALBERTOSAURUS   TYRANNOSAURUS   LAMBEOSAURUS

Other animals shared the world with the dinosaurs and some still live today. There were lots of insects around, so you'd see ants, cockroaches, mosquitoes, and dragonflies (some with three-foot wingspans). There were also prehistoric snakes, alligators, turtles, sharks, and lizards that all looked a lot like their modern-day relatives.

45

Dinosaurs lived on Earth for about 177 million years. Then, over a short time span, they all vanished—all the dinosaurs and many other life-forms we now know only from fossils. What happened to them?

Paleontologists think that a giant chunk of rock and ice from space, called a meteor, crashed into Earth, throwing up great clouds of dust and dirt, which made Earth colder and darker. This would have kept plants from growing, and the plant-eating dinosaurs would have had a hard time finding things to eat. If the plant-eaters starved, the meat-eating dinosaurs that preyed on them would have starved too.

This is one theory and there are many more. There are other questions too. Why didn't turtles or fish or crocodiles that lived along with the dinosaurs become extinct? Why are cockroaches and sharks still around, but not dinosaurs? Maybe you will find those answers someday.

47

BIBLIOGRAPHY

Bakker, Robert T., Ph.D. *The Dinosaur Heresies: New Theories Unlocking the Mystery of the Dinosaurs and Their Extinction*. New York: William Morrow, 1986.

Carpenter, Kenneth, Karl F. Hirsch, and John R. Horner, eds. *Dinosaur Eggs and Babies*. New York: Cambridge University Press, 1996.

Dixon, Dougal, Barry Cox, R.J.G. Savage, and Brian Gardiner, eds. *The Macmillan Illustrated Encyclopedia of Dinosaurs and Prehistoric Animals*. New York: Collier Books, 1988.

Lambert, David, and the Diagram Group, eds. *The Dinosaur Data Book*. New York: Avon Books, 1990.

Norman, David, Ph.D. *Dinosaur!* New York: Prentice Hall, 1991.

Paul, Gregory S. *Predatory Dinosaurs of the World*. New York: Simon & Schuster, 1988.

INDEX